INTIMATE SEX
More Often

Includes 75 Enlightening
Tips plus 30 Ways for
Men to Last Longer!

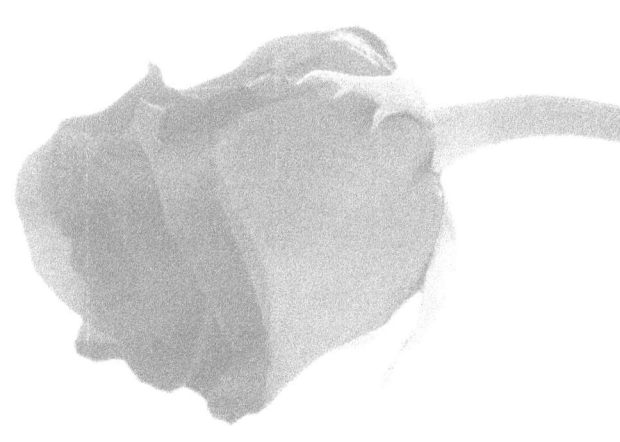

Dave Robin

Diamond Publications
Lakewood, Colorado

Copyright © 2015 Dave Robin.
Manufactured in the United States of America. All rights reserved. No part of this book may be reproduced in any form or by any electronic or mechanical means including information storage and retrieval systems without the permission in writing from the publisher, except by a reviewer, who may quote brief passages in a review.

Published by Diamond Publications
Lakewood, CO

For book sales contact: www.IntimateSexMoreOften.com or contact Dave@IntimateSexMoreOften.com.

Although the author and publisher have made every effort to insure the accuracy and completeness of information contained in this book, we assume no responsibility for errors, inaccuracies, omissions, or any inconsistency herein. Any slights of people, places, or organizations are unintentional.

> Robin, Dave
> Intimate Sex, More Often/Dave Robin—1sted.
> P cm.
> Includes index
> Printed in the U.S.A.

ISBN: 978-0-9626776-0-1
0-9626776-0-4
15 16 17 18 19   0 9 8 7 6 5 4 3 2 1

Relationships, Romance, Self-help, Sexuality—United States.

Edited by Aimee Bennett, Fagan Business Communications
Aimee@FaganBusinessCommunications.com

Design, layout and production by Pam McKinnie,
Concepts Unlimited
ConceptsUnlimited@Estreet.com
ConceptsUnlimitedInc.com

Dedication

To you, the reader, and doctors, sex
therapists, educators and counselors,
celebrities, my family, and friends

Today
Yesterday
Tomorrow

Acknowledgements

Many people contributed their thoughts, time, and talents to this book. My appreciation is extended to the key individuals who assisted me with the writing, editing, layout, and production of this book (as well as two previous critically acclaimed best-selling business books): Aimee Bennett and Pam McKinnie.

I am especially grateful to the women I have known over the years, and to all the men, women, physicians, sex therapists, counselors, educators, and other experts who have provided insight and ideas as I've compiled my information. Their input has made all the difference, and I thank them.

And a special thank you goes to members of AASECT (the American Association of Sexuality Educators, Counselors, and Therapists) whose guidance has added credibility to the suggestions contained in this book.

Table of Contents

Dedication..i
Acknowledgements..iii

Preface..1
Introduction..5
   Take control of your sexual future.....................8
   The dirty word..9
   Good times...11
Section One: The Nifty 50.........................13
Before Sex: 50 Ways to Create the Atmosphere
Chapter 1: Be True to Yourself.............. 17
   1. *Be faithful*..17
   2. *In your partner you trust*..........................17
   3. *Be careful*..17
   4. *Be caring and sincere*................................18
   5. *Never fake it*...18
Chapter 2: Educate Yourself.........................21
   6. *Adopt a willingness to learn*......................21
   7. *Keep your clothes on*..................................22
   8. *Tell him (her) what you want*...................22
   9. *Fore! Play*..23
   10. *Ladies first*...28
   11. *Learn to multiply*.....................................28

Table of Contents

   12. Embrace female ejaculation......29
   13. Lube up......31
   14. Find the G-spot......32
   15. Many roads lead to the same place......32
   16. Massage your partner......33
   17. The Big O and The Big C......34
   18. Play......34

Chapter 3: Take Good Care of Yourself......37
   19. Have a (non-alcoholic) drink......37
   20. Shower, manicure, and shave......37
   21. Time for a shave? Talk about it......39
   22. Treat all hairs equally......39
   23. Skip the incense, fragrances, perfume, and cologne......40

Chapter 4: Clear Your Mind and Schedule......43
   24. Remain objective!......43
   25. Dismiss the elephants in the room......43
   26. Let go of expectations......44
   27. Don't expect perfection......44
   28. Accept your appearance......45
   29. Accept your partner's appearance......45
   30. Take time......46

Table of Contents

31. Don't settle 46
32. Take nature in stride 46
33. It's not personal 47
34. Have a good – time even if you're tired 47

Chapter 5: Be Better Prepared 49
35. Think it through 49
36. Become an advance man (or woman) 49
37. Wash, rinse, dry 50

Chapter 6: Spruce Up the Bedroom 53
38. Do not disturb 53
39. Keep it comfy 53
40. Strip (the bed) 54
41. Treat yourself like a king or queen 54
42. Beware of bedposts and rails 54
43. Once upon a mattress 54
44. Invest in quality bedding 55
45. Keep it clean 56
46. Turn off the noise 56
47. Turn on the lights 58
48. It's good to be seen and heard 58
49. Make time stand still 59
50. Keep it handy 59

Table of Contents

Section Two: During Sex..................61
Enhance the Experience
Chapter 7: 30 Reliable Ways to Last 4 Times Longer..................63
   51. Be master of your domain..................63
Chapter 8: Explore..................81
   52. Position yourself..................81
   53. Your lucky number..................81
   54. Experiment..................83
   55. Head-to-toe..................84
   56. A couple that plays together..................84
   57. Sweat..................84
Chapter 9: Check In..................87
   58. What's up?..................87
   59. Fantasize..................87
Chapter 10: Relax..................89
   60. Operate on autopilot..................89
   61. Take a breath..................89
   62. (Don't) mind-read..................89
   63. It's not everything..................89
   64. Come together (or not)..................90
   65. Lose your inhibitions..................90

Table of Contents

Section Three: After Sex................................93
Finish Strong
Chapter 11: Bask in the Afterglow...............95
  66. *Engage in afterplay*...................................95
  67. *Go again*..95
  68. *15 minutes of fame*...................................95
  69. *Snuggle*..96
  70. *Pack a toothbrush*....................................96
  71. *Love means never having to say you're
      sorry*..96
  72. *Sleep naked*...96
  73. *Just a touch*..97
  74. *24 hours*..97
  75. *The day after*..97
Afterword..99

Preface

If you've watched late-night TV, or been to a comedy club, you know that comedians often make fun of men and pity women in their sexual jokes. Like many men, I took some of these comments to heart in my early dating years. Add in an experience with an angry woman venting about men and I knew I needed to become better informed on sex.

While I'd done my share of reading, watching videos, and listening to audiotapes over the years, a divorce from a wonderful woman after 24 years sealed the decision to update my views on sex. I listened to women carefully, read voraciously about sex, romance, and relationships, added selected books to my library, and ordered new educational videos. As I broadened my knowledge, focus, and attitude, I grew in confidence. And as I put what I was learning into play, I quickly found again that my insights were well received and appreciated in the dating world, enhancing every encounter and every relationship.

It also occurred to me that, for the first time in more than 20 years, I could design my bedroom in any way I wanted, making it more comfortable and aesthetically pleasing. As I thought through and researched the components of the room, I began to understand better the experience I sought. I realized that this new perspective – and attention to detail – would not only benefit me, but the women in my life.

So I continued to listen, read, study, and learn. Moving forward from the comfortable "bedroom design" experience, I still had questions, but was starting to see that what women wanted wasn't so different from what I wanted. At the end of the day, we all wanted a comfortable, inviting, connected relationship in a safe environment, with a partner who was open to learning and communicating.

Over time, I realized that I had a very different attitude on sex and relationships than other men. As time went on, this was reinforced by the positive feedback I received from my female partners.

Yet, writing a book on intimate sex was the furthest thing from my mind – in fact, wasn't even in my mind – for the first 55 of my 60 years. I was happily pursuing my marriage, career, and community activities.

Then, during a terrific two-year relationship with a wonderful, open, sexually confident woman, I started to reflect on what made the sex in that relationship so fulfilling. It seemed as if we had the kind of relationship other couples were looking for – and sometimes had difficulty actualizing. As I moved from that relationship to others, I consistently received feedback on how my partners' physical and emotional reactions extended beyond anything they had experienced – and were literally "the stuff dreams were made of." In an effort to discover what made these relationships so fulfilling, I began to jot down notes about what seemed to enhance the relationship. Ultimately I realized that my "notes" had value for others and those initial thoughts evolved into this book.

Having intimate sex more often is not entirely about mouthwash, the thread count of your sheets, or any other single "tip." However, over time I discovered that as I consciously acted on each of the tips shared in this guide, my experience of intimate sex evolved. I became more comfortable with myself and my partner. I learned to communicate, to ask questions, and to ask for permission. The more I communicated, the more confident I became. The more questions my partner asked, the more confident she became. Positive responses led to more discussion, which helped eliminate insecurities and resulted in even more confidence. Trust was built and sex became not only intimate, but it brought me (and my partners) a feeling of what can only be described as joy and inner peace. **Intimate, fulfilling sex evolves over time. It grows on you and eventually you refuse to accept anything less.**

Along with experts on sex and relationships, I believe that my observations and experiences contain value for others.

The result of my journey is this guide.

Introduction

The road to intimate sex is about getting to know your partner — emotionally, physically, mentally, and for many, spiritually — in ways you haven't before, about shaping a new attitude and creating new experiences. Ideally, you'll do this, and read this guide, with your partner so that the two of you can evolve on a mutual path together.

Keep in mind that the tips are meant to serve as starting points for communication, so you may find yourselves venturing off into other topics. Since great communication is the mainstay of great sex, go ahead and pursue these — and return to the book later.

You also may find that the two of you experience disagreement in certain areas, or find tips one or both of you are not comfortable discussing. Think it through and try to talk about the issue. Or at least ask yourselves why it's difficult to do so. The point is not to agree with everything in the book, but to talk with your partner, broaden your perspective, and make changes that will lead you to your own experiences of intimate sex more often.

The 75 simple tips in the book apply to you whether you have a little extra padding or a big stomach; or whether you are short, tall, young, or old. The book has tried to cover almost every element of the sexual experience – no matter how trivial it might seem – in order to satisfy an entire range of readers. Intimate sex can be yours more often. It takes only willingness, thought, attitude, preparation, and very little money on your part.

You can put a few tips into use at any time, and you'll find you can put most things you'll read into play tonight. You, the reader, can decide which areas merit your energy and attention. Being as honest as you can will move you down the road to intimate sex more often and more quickly… And you'll benefit from the results for the rest of your life.

Introduction

If you're unsure your partner is ready to embark on the journey with you, you can read this book on your own and gradually put into play the ideas presented without his/her express knowledge. You may find your partner (happily) noticing the results and becoming curious. Just make sure s/he is aware that the changes are arising from the book and not due to an external relationship or affair!

Take control of your sexual future... and begin reaping the rewards

Fact: Intimate sex more often is not going to happen on its own.

Fact: Intimate sex more often can and will happen with a little effort.

No matter where you are in your relationship, and no matter what type of relationship you are in, **I want you to experience what it's like to walk hand-in-hand with your partner with the unspoken glow that others can see.** In part it comes from trust, acceptance, understanding, and caring. I want you to experience intimate sex – and experience it more often.

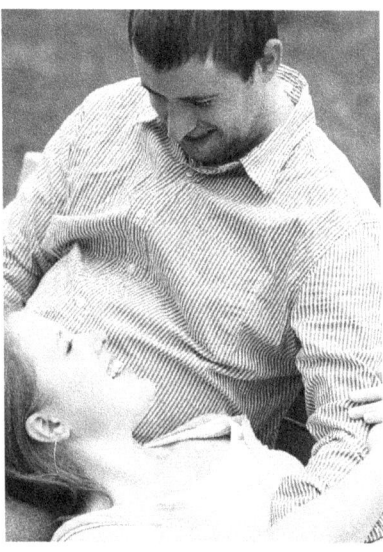

Introduction

The key is in "partnership." This book is intended for those in a relationship, of almost any type or duration. Those in mature relationships will find reminders of things they know but may have forgotten – and quite a few new items to enhance the experience. For those whose relationships have fallen into monotony or become stagnant, the material in this book will break the ice. New couples and newlyweds will find fresh perspective on their views and eye-opening tips. Every reader will come away with new ideas, new communication skills, and an improved sex life. If you find words you're not familiar with, this is a good opportunity to look up the formal definition.

The Dirty Word...Communication

Many men in America have learned to cringe at the word. They dread long sessions of discussing feelings without a tangible end. But in this book, we'll liken communication to dining at a great restaurant. If you went to the restaurant week after week and never told the waiter what you wanted, you'd likely get water, the soup of the day, a standard salad, and a specialty of the day or whatever main dish the kitchen had to spare that day. Not bad, but not great. With a little direct communication on your part, your dining experience will be magnified. Similarly, we'll focus on the way you talk about sex – what you want and need – with your partner. Men generally find when they can talk about sex first, communicating about other areas of life becomes easier.

By putting into play the tips in this book, you'll find you'll strengthen your overall communication and relationship with your partner. You will find a real or deeper love you've not experienced before. And you'll find yourself possessing a different attitude. You'll look forward to creating experiences rather than just having sex. **You'll likely find that the more, and more easily, you can talk about sex, the easier it becomes to talk about finances, disciplining the children, taking out the trash, and other household chores.** With a changed outlook and perspective, you may even find better communication and rapport with in-laws, co-workers, and extended family.

Good times

If you really put into play some of the tips in the book, you'll experience more good times and more fun. Climaxes are only the bonus. What awaits you will redefine and reshape your personal "high" feelings. **Combine your best workout, all your endorphins, and your unarticulated dreams, and you'll come close to the inner feeling of personal satisfaction that is possible.**

You will be able to reach new depths – or develop intimacy you didn't even know was available. **You'll learn to become aware of just how many distractions exist in sexual experiences, and how eliminating them brings a continuity never before experienced.**

Many shy people also have found that learning how to communicate more openly with their partners about sex helps them become more open and less introverted in other areas of their lives.

Section One

The Nifty 50

Before Sex: *50 Ways to Create the Atmosphere*

There's a good reason this book contains far more tips on what to do before sex than during sex: Sex is more about attitude and creating intimate moments than actually "getting it on." Intimacy includes sexuality, but is much more than sexual intercourse. To initiate, maintain, and enhance sexual desire and fulfillment, you'll need a variety of ways to connect and re-connect. These range from flirting (yes, even with a long-time partner) and affectionate touching to non-genital play and foreplay – and then intercourse and the intimate time afterward.

Much of what you'll read in the Nifty 50 has to do with attitude, preparation, and communication. Women sometimes believe (or want to believe) that men somehow know instinctively how to satisfy them, how to treat them, and how to initiate and have great sex. But as best as I can tell, **most men have never been taught and**

don't know how to have intimate sex. Often what they learn from parents, the locker room, or friends over a beer is of little use. The reality is that learning together, as a couple, is the only way to achieve great sex. And you learn by being open and communicating.

Women sometimes believe (or want to believe) that men somehow know instinctively how to satisfy them, how to treat them, and how to initiate and have great sex. But as best as I can tell, most men have never been taught and don't know how to have sex.

It's my opinion that the longer two people have been together without real communication about sex, the more challenging it will be. Intimate communication is far from impossible, though, and the effort will pay off in ways neither could expect. For those whose sex lives may have become somewhat routine, a wealth of information, ideas, and resources will help move sex lives forward. Putting the concepts in this book into practice will benefit your relationship for life.

Try implementing a few of the tips when you can. Many will require you to think and make a few adjustments. Most are suggestions for one-time changes, and many are things you can put into play spontaneously. The more positive feedback you receive, and the more positive, open attitude you maintain, the more likely you'll be to take action on more of the tips. You'll be surprised at the affirming feedback you receive, and how your confidence will soar!

You build trust – specifically relating to sexual trust – only over time, and through discussions of your wants, needs, insecurities, fears, experience, inexperience, turn-ons, and turn-offs.

Chapter One
Be True to Yourself

1. Be faithful

You've heard it before, but I'm here to tell you it's the number one component to great sex: Be faithful to whomever you're with. You'll have no guilt and no thoughts that impede your pursuit of intimate sex, more often.

2. In your partner you trust

Just as you must be faithful, for intimate sex, more often, you must trust your partner. You build trust – specifically relating to sexual trust – only over time, and through discussions of your wants, needs, insecurities, fears, experience, inexperience, turn-ons, and turn-offs.

3. Be careful

Remember that we live in an age where "being careful" takes on life-and-death proportions. Sexually transmitted diseases are real and are serious. No matter what you learn from this book, first and foremost is the health and safety of you and your partner. Physical trust isn't blind trust, so make sure you and your partner have been appropriately tested and proceed accordingly. Open up and talk it out – then you'll be on the way to trust and intimate sex, more often.

4. Be caring and sincere with your partner

If you don't truly care for each other, sex turns into an unemotional, manual act. Intimate sex is physically, emotionally, mentally, and for many, spiritually fulfilling. It's a two way street. One side can't just take and not give. With a genuine, caring attitude, two people will feel more secure, confident, and free to act with no inhibitions.

5. Never fake it

That's right – never. Men and women tend to fake orgasms for many reasons: to get sex over with, to prop up their partner's feelings, to help their partner climax, or because they're hurt, tired, or bored. Don't do it. It will damage your credibility, tear down trust being built, and bottom line, if you follow what's in this book, you won't need to fake it. Not faking it is going to take a little effort in how you communicate with your partner. It's worth it.

*O*pen up and talk it out – then you'll be on the way to trust and intimate sex, more often.

Think about your greatest passion: Geology, running, cooking?...Great sex can be just as much fun.

Chapter Two
Educate Yourself

6. **Adopt a willingness to learn**

You're off to a good start, because if you're here reading this book, you already have proven that you want to learn more! Interestingly, **most people spend more time preparing for a vacation than they do on their sexual lives.**

Think about your greatest passion. Geology? Running? Cooking? Whatever it is, how much do you know about it? How much time and attention do you spend studying it, learning about it, reading about it? Probably a good deal. Your sex life is just as deserving! Do you have three or more additional educational CDs, DVDs, or books on sex in your library? This isn't referring to porn movies, videos, or Internet sites, but rather well-written materials. If you don't have these, pick a subject you're curious about, buy a book, CD or DVD. Be careful about online information. Check out the source.

7. Keep your clothes on

A critical factor in maintaining a woman's sexual desire is the attraction and lust that the partner feels for her. If you want your sex life to rev up and stay healthy, do things that make you like and admire each other when you have your clothes on. Both partners will be happier and more confident.

8. Tell him (her) what you need

Begin discussing what you want and like (and don't want or like) *before* you engage in your sexual experience. That may be a day before, the night before, or the hour before. Why? You build anticipation, you build trust, and you build a solid foundation. Make sure to come to agreement on anything new you'd like before trying it out.

Most of us are not comfortable completely expressing ourselves. Whether we learned this in childhood or later in life, it can hinder our sexual experiences. Unless you feel comfortable and safe – emotionally, mentally, physically, spiritually – with your partner, you can't effectively start talking about the things you want and need.

For many couples, getting to that point actually can come from starting to talk more and opening up. Maybe you'd like to experiment with a certain sex toy. Maybe you want a certain kind of stroke during foreplay. Whatever it is, allow trust to build by starting to talk more and bringing these things to your partner's attention.

You'll likely be surprised by the positive feedback you receive. Yet if your partner doesn't want to try something, respect his or her decision. Move on, and perhaps bring it up again at some later point. As you grow together in experience, you'll each share and stretch just a bit more. (If you truly do not feel comfortable, or have significant concerns, it's important to seek professional counsel.)

9. Fore Play!

Women may think two hours of foreplay only happens in their dreams. They're tired of six-minute foreplay. Men, on the other hand, often shudder to think of "holding off" for two hours and consider foreplay a brief requisite for moving forward.

Men may be surprised to learn that while they need only six to seven minutes to climax, women average about 25 minutes. Many women may have a lower biological urge for the release of sexual tension than men, and may begin their sexual experiences in sexual "neutrality." However, foreplay often can move them to a state of seeking sexual contact and stimulation.

While it's not always possible to engage in hours of foreplay, try it sometime. Or try thinking about foreplay with a little different attitude.

What it is – and what it's not

Important to any discussion of foreplay is an understanding of what it is – and isn't. Defined, foreplay is a set of intimate psychological and physical acts, meant to build sexual arousal. It's not merely a mechanical matter of stimulation. In its initial stages, foreplay is often subtle, verbal, and involves other non-physical behavior that a person uses to signal sexual interest.

Verbal foreplay includes sexual compliments, comments with double entendre, erotic talk, and conversations about sexual acts and desires – as

Men may be surprised to learn that while they need only six to seven minutes to climax, women average about 25 minutes. Many women may have a lower biological urge for the release of sexual tension than men, and may begin their sexual experiences in sexual "neutrality." However, foreplay often can move them to a state of seeking sexual contact and stimulation.

long as it's all in a positive tone and never demeaning. We all know of non-verbal, non-physical foreplay behavior such as licking or biting one's lips, holding another's gaze, engaging in playfulness, and other gestures. Physical and verbal foreplay lowers inhibitions and increases the emotional comfort level between partners. Foreplay also goes both ways – It's not just something men do "for" women. However, foreplay can be especially helpful for women, as it stimulates vaginal lubrication, which allows penetration to take place more comfortably. It's also important to remember that women can climax (or be truly satisfied without climaxing) without penetration.

Getting Started

By creating anticipation, extended foreplay heightens excitement, and gives each partner new confidence and enjoyment. Not sure where to start? **Tuck a private note into a purse or wallet** so your partner sees it on a busy day, or leave a voice-mail message letting your partner know you're thinking about him or her. While there's no need to set the stage this way before every sexual encounter (where's the spontaneity in that?), it's a fun, simple, effective means of foreplay.

Physically, begin with touching the extremities (not genitals) of your partner's body. Lavish attention on your partner's whole body during physical foreplay and get to know his or her pleasure zones. Build your own couple style. Whatever you do, make sure you don't allow anything in which you have no interest. Avoid "bartering" with your partner ("if you do this to me, I'll do something

Educate Yourself

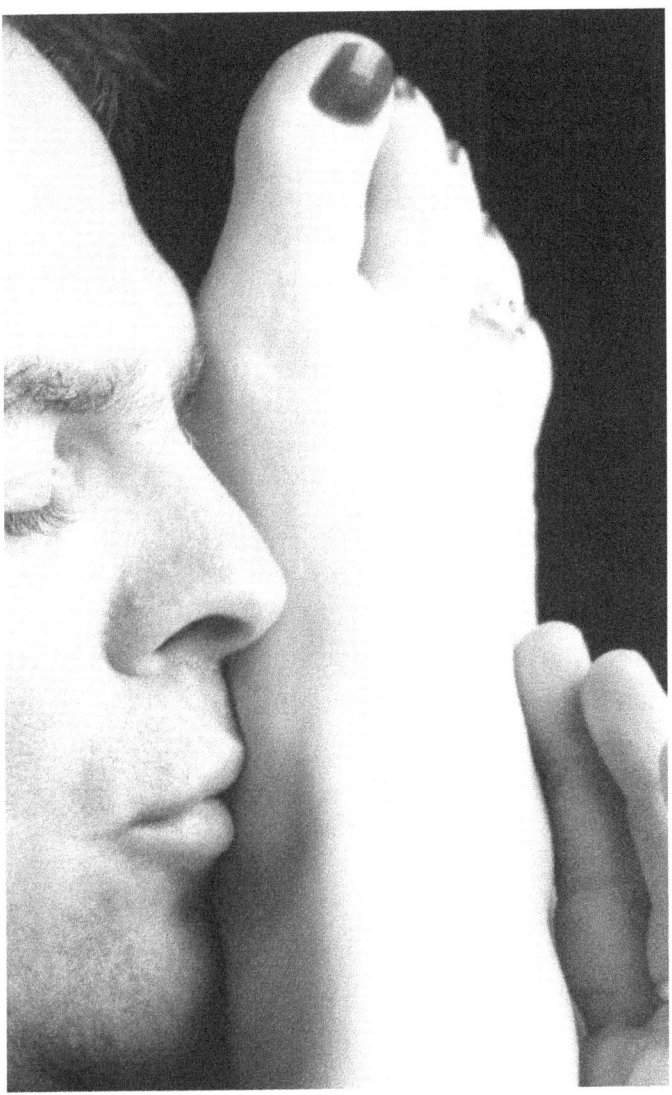

for you"), but take time, get talking, and experiment.

10. Ladies first

Simply put, men who go off too soon will lose out on a lot of fun and intimacy. Start with learning to hold off. This skill will help build a stronger relationship. (*See Chapter 7*)

11. Learn how to multiply

Your orgasms, that is. If you don't know how to have multiple orgasms now, relax. Achieving multiples is a learned skill and natural extension of the arousal process – for both men and women. Try different positions that work for both you and your partner, and talk about it with each other. Learn to let him/her know when to stop – **or not stop** – a particular action that's working for you. Agree on a body signal, whether it's a certain touch or particular moan, to communicate what you need or like.

For those who are reading this and thinking that women have a hard enough time with one orgasm, let alone more, think again. Women can climax in many ways, even through something as simple as a kiss. Many women don't recognize, physically, what is happening with their bodies throughout early arousal. How many orgasms can a woman have? There's no limit. It's simply when the woman doesn't want any more.

Be aware that the ability to achieve multiple orgasms can be affected by stress, diet, smoking, depression, anger, and some cultural and religious practices. Otherwise, keep experimenting and keep talking – always with an open, caring attitude.

12. Embrace female ejaculation

A subject of much debate, and infrequent open discussion, female ejaculation (also called squirting, spraying, or gushing) can and does happen. It's commonly believed that a clear, odorless, colorless fluid produced in the spongy G-spot penetrates the urethra during vaginal climax. The fluid is not urine and does not come from the bladder. It is possible that a cup or more of fluid can be produced. Only a fraction of women (and fewer men) are familiar with female ejaculation. An even smaller number of women have experienced it, but for those who have, female ejaculation is often a step above and beyond orgasm. It's another learned behavior, so with a little study and effort, it's closer than most couples know.

Achieving this natural experience – wonderful for both parties – usually starts with kissing, then breast fondling, fingering the vagina and vulva, then penetration. In terms of positions, many women do better sitting on top, but each couple is different. If and when you or your partner do experience female ejaculation, pay attention to your position and what you did to lead up to it for future reference. And, by continuing the action that led up to it, the woman may experience multiple streams.

Many women hold back, or block ejaculation intentionally, as they confuse it with the feeling that they need to urinate. Just as with men, it's impossible to urinate and ejaculate at the same time. Female ejaculation often causes the woman to spontaneously eject the penis. If this happens, resuming penetration will normally prolong the woman's sexual experience.

All these reactions are normal (check with a knowledgeable doctor, counselor, sex therapist, sex educator, or other informed professional if you're not convinced). Talking this over with your partner will be reassuring to both of you, and you'll become more comfortable with the idea.

13. Lube up

This book does not evaluate or endorse types of lubrication. Just be aware that different types of lubrication products are available for different purposes, all designed to reduce friction, dryness, and soreness. A few guidelines will truly make your sexual experience significantly better.

- Don't use petroleum jelly lubricants. They are difficult to wash out and may irritate the vaginal lining and change vaginal chemistry, increasing risk of infection. They also destroy latex and should never be used with condoms, diaphragms or cervical caps. Finally, petroleum lubricants may stain fabric.

- Learn about, experiment with, and find which of the many brands and types of water-based lubrication on the market work best for you; some women will experience a negative reaction to some ingredients.

- Use lubricant on your condom (if using one) as well as in the woman's vagina. The use of lubricants is often underestimated for enhancing the sexual experience and making it more comfortable.

14. Find the G-spot

Aaah, the much-contested G-spot. Some contend that most women have one, although it takes time and experimentation to locate and stimulate it. Location: According to experts, it's often between the 11 and 1 o'clock positions, behind the clitoris. Stimulation: Pressure, with one or two fingers (as if you were gesturing toward your palm) sometimes works.

15. Understand that many roads lead to the same place

Climaxes and orgasms are produced in several ways. For women, climaxes can happen through clitoral stimulation, penal penetration, direct stimulation of the G-spot, and fingering (ranging from gently pulling on and caressing the lips to vaginal penetration). For men, climax can happen through penetration, stroking, or anal stimulation. Often, lubrication can add to the experience.

Many women prefer fingering to penetration; only about 30 percent of women will climax with penetration alone (which may be because not all positions will stimulate the G-spot). Whichever method you select, be aware that each produces a different type of climax. Each person is different; each type of climax is satisfying in different ways. Also, be aware that many women may experience climax or orgasm before penetration.

16. Massage your partner

While most people know how sensuous and relaxing getting a massage can be, **few people understand how intense and intimate it can be for the partner who gives the massage**. Not only is massage a great form of foreplay, it shows you

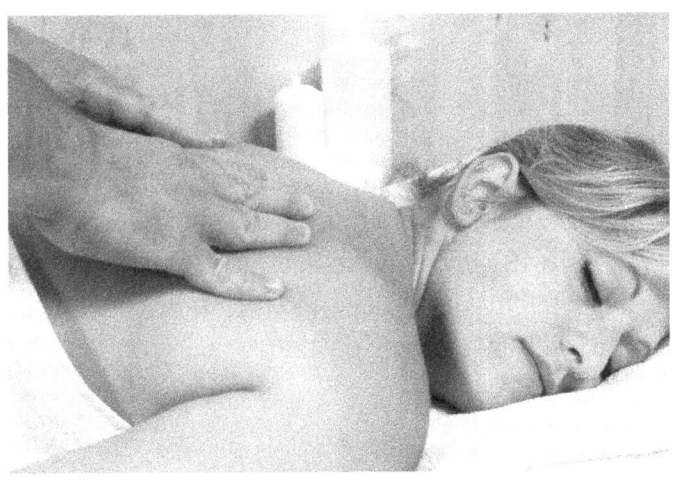

care, helps remove inhibitions, and can even bring on a climax or orgasm by itself.

Women's sexual arousal develops after initial sensual contact. While a man's sexual desire develops through physical drive, a woman's develops from her receptivity to gentle, relaxed sensual touching. Massage is an excellent way to begin this touching that can then lead to emotional closeness, affection, sensuality, and eroticism.

17. Learn the difference between The Big O and The Big C

Some experts believe orgasm is a full-body experience that includes the brain. Climax is simply the physical reaction of the genitals being satisfied.

18. Play

Incorporating toys, food, props, and other accessories can prove interesting and useful for your sexual experience – when **used sparingly** or occasionally. Know what is available, choose a few about which you're curious, and talk them over accordingly with your partner.

Here's a partial list of possible accessories to consider:
a. DVDs
b. CDs
c. Magazines
d. Handcuffs
e. Rose petals
f. Sex swing
g. Feathers
h. Vibrator
i. Dildo
j. Selected clothing (something other than white underwear for men!)
k. Blindfolds
l. Flavored lubricants

Intimate Sex More Often

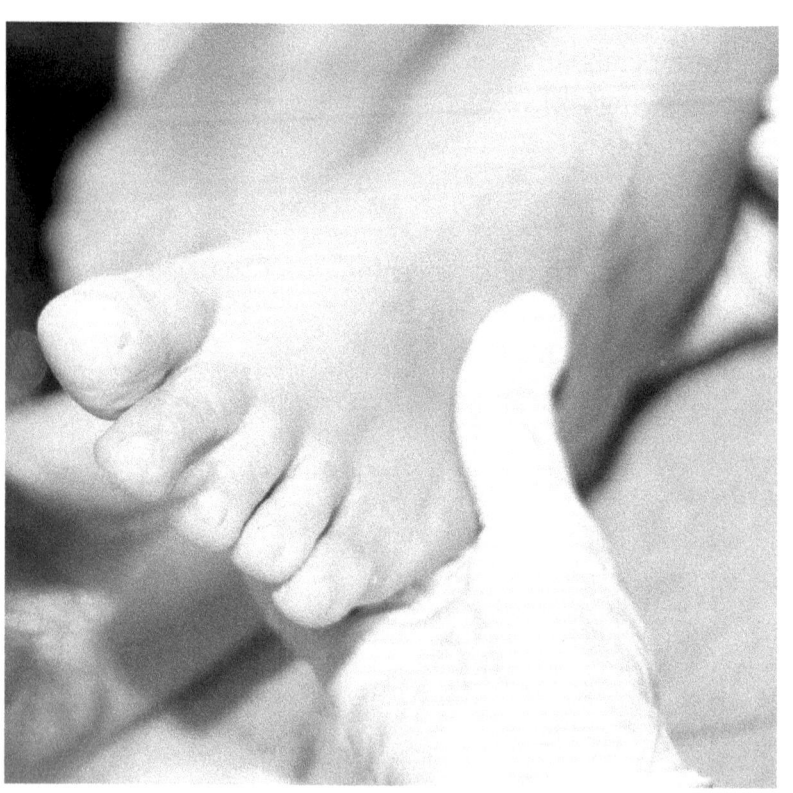

Chapter Three
Take Good Care of Yourself

19. Have a (non-alcoholic) drink

While alcohol can heighten a sexual experience, keep in mind that the times when that happens are few and far between. Both partners need to be perfectly in sync with mood, desire, and impact of alcohol. Even if it does happen, your sexual experience will be shorter lived.

The fact is that alcohol is a depressant, not a stimulant. Alcohol deadens the sexual experience, or at best, makes the experience more difficult. Don't rely on it – rely instead on communicating with your partner and experiencing the moment in full.

20. Shower, manicure, and shave

Often, men and women don't realize how far a little extra personal care can go in the bedroom. Taking good care of yourself improves confidence, eliminates many common worries, and will absolutely enrich your sexual experience.

Shower or bathe before you get into bed, even if you haven't planned on having sex. You never know what will happen. Women may find that using a low-PH soap minimizes vaginal irritation.

Shave. A woman's shaved and smooth legs – and a man's shaved face/trimmed beard – can do more than one might expect for a partner. Men might even find it handy to keep a battery-operated shaver in the car.

Keep mouthwash and paper cups at each sink in the home for easy access. Or keep it in a decanter with a spout close by (it's more attractive and faster than conventional bottles of mouthwash). Keep a travel-size unit in the car.

If you're without mouthwash or a toothbrush, you can swish and swallow toothpaste.

Place washcloths at each sink to cleanse private areas before sex. You'll feel more confident.

Get a monthly manicure and a pedicure. **Men, this means you, too.** The reason men's manicures and pedicures are becoming more popular nationwide is that men are finding they are more confident, look better, and please their partners more. Choose a shop carefully for cleanliness. Men, if you're uncomfortable, ask the manager for a private location within the salon.

21. Time for a shave? Talk about it.

We get haircuts, shave underarms, legs, and faces, so why not consider extending this care to the pubic area? Reflect and talk this over with your partner. You may make some different decisions on shaving or waxing than you would have otherwise. A word of caution: Do your homework before using a razor; there are precautions and techniques that apply specifically to pubic areas.

22. Treat all hairs equally

If you choose to keep your pubic hair, be consistent. You can create a distraction when your latest hairdo is blond, but your pubic hair is brunette. However, you should be very cautious about dying pubic hair. The only dyes that might be safe are organic dyes.

23. Skip the incense, fragrances, perfume, and cologne

Scents can distract your partner or remind one or both of you of prior experiences. Rather than relive the past (however great it was), focus on creating and experiencing the present. If you find yourself in this situation, think it through, and/or talk it over with your partner. And remember that some people are actually allergic to certain perfumes and colognes. Finally, if you do use a scent, remember that it is to be discovered, not noticed.

Taking good care of yourself improves confidence, eliminates many common worries, and will absolutely enrich your sexual experience.

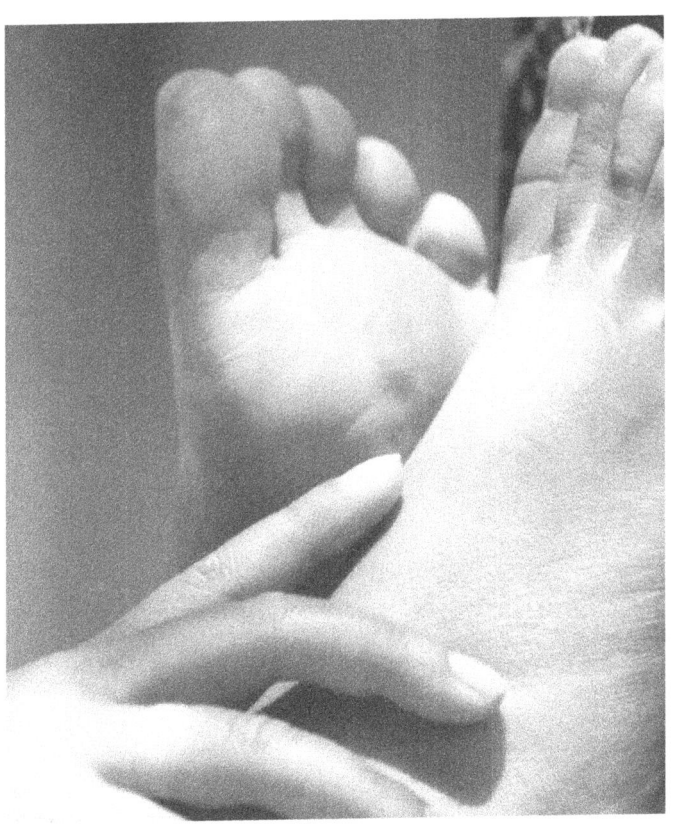

Dismiss the elephant in the room.

Chapter Four
Clear Your Mind and Your Schedule

24. Remain objective!

Rather than taking any comment to heart, try hard to remain objective in your discussions, knowing that you and your partner will disagree on various issues. Treat what you and your partner discuss with sensitivity and privacy in an emotionally safe environment.

25. Dismiss the elephants in the room

You know those elephants – the mental issues that can get in the way of fully expressing oneself. Bring up your own and ask your partner to address his or her issues. Create a safe atmosphere. Hold, hug, and really talk. Doing these things will allow you to be "in the moment." You'll both feel like a huge burden has been lifted and that you've done your best to leave the world at the bedroom door.

26. Let go of expectations

With only anticipation, not expectation, you will rarely if ever be disappointed. You'll find yourself more fully open to your partner and to creating your own unique experience. And if something doesn't work out, no one feels awkward or guilty later.

27. Don't expect perfection

Whether it's sex or riding a bike, trying something new won't always be terrific the first few times. Keep a positive attitude. The more you communicate with your partner, and the more you try different things, the more you'll learn, the more you'll trust, and the greater your satisfaction will be. And always remember: If something is happening that you don't like or with which you're not comfortable, speak up. It's about communicating to find what works for the **two** of you. The key in sexual desire is to establish and reinforce a cycle of positive anticipation and pleasurable sexual experiences. Men, in particular, need to understand that they'll lessen both the quality and quantity of sexual experiences if they view sex as a test or if they tell themselves that anything less than a "perfect" sexual performance means they are less of a man.

28. Accept your appearance

You've heard it before, and you'll hear it again – because it's true. **You *don't* need to look like a model.** Your body is only about one percent of who you are. You *do* need to accept yourself and appreciate all you have going for you. It's all about attitude (again). Learn to concentrate on the good things so that you can look in the mirror and like what you see. You'll be more relaxed and gain peace of mind. And know that almost without exception, the things about which you may be insecure – weight, stretch marks, cellulite, blemishes, scars, moles, or effects of gravity – are non-issues for your partner.

29. Accept your partner's appearance

Develop an attitude of being happy with your partner for who s/he is. That includes appearance. Sometimes, though, we may want to look at our partners in a different context. In foreplay, for instance, a man can use his penis to rub the back of his partner's knee, elbow, or underarm. The visual and

physical experience allows both the man and woman to think of every part of the body as sexual.

30. Take time

Time is the greatest gift. Everyone has a busy schedule. And not every time you have sex can you take unlimited amounts of time. But to achieve intimate sex more often, slow down and work toward an open-ended timeline when possible. Taking the urgency out of sex opens up possibilities and eliminates distractions. Even if you do have limited time, remember that it's better to have a quality, sensual, and relaxing experience rather than trying to force a climax.

31. Don't settle

If you're chasing sex, you'll never achieve truly great sex. Work toward sex with your partner through caring, attention, and progression toward love (if you're not already there). Seek an experience. Sex is different for each person, so don't rely on assumptions or generalizations.

32. Take nature in stride

Menstrual periods, sneezing, gas, different smells, and using the restroom all are normal human functions that will no doubt occur during your sexual experiences. Continue to build trust by talking about them up-front – or just laugh about them – and then put these things behind you so you can focus on a unique experience between just the two of you.

33. "It's not personal"

If your partner says "no," realize that it's usually for any number of reasons, many of which may have nothing to do with you. It may have something to do with an elephant (see # 25). Instead of quietly retreating (and sulking), inquire. You may be surprised to find a welcome reception to your interest, and in the process, build communication and trust.

34. Have a good time – even if you're tired

Face it. We're not perfectly rested all the time. Realize your body can and will respond effectively even when tired. Good sleep is important, but it's also possible to have great sex when you're tired out. Just let your partner know that you're willing, but may need to be a bit more passive. He or she will appreciate it, and you, all the more.

Writing a short love note, flirting, or making a call to let your partner know s/he is in your thoughts and teasing with expressions of what the night (or day) might bring heightens anticipation.

Chapter Five
Be Better Prepared

35. Think it through

Here's one area where the thought really does count. Remembering what your partner likes, preparing for what you want, and thinking about what works for you and your partner – whether it's a certain touch, or a particular accessory s/he occasionally likes – will bring you closer to intimate sex, more often.

36. Become an advance man (or woman)

Letting your partner know you're interested in sex tonight, tomorrow, the weekend (or whenever) builds anticipation, speaks volumes about your care for the other person, and increases desire and enthusiasm. Writing a short love note, flirting, or making a call to let your partner know s/he is in your thoughts and teasing with expressions of what the night (or day) might bring heightens anticipation that much more. In general, the more notice, the better. But even just 10 minutes' notice allows for contemplation, excitement, and preparation. (Refer also to Tip #8.)

37. Wash, rinse, dry

Worrying about something getting dirty takes away from the experience, as it will distract you from being in the moment. If you have concerns about a particular item of clothing or bedding getting dirty, take it off, store it, or move it. Relax. That's what washing machines and dry cleaners are for! Putting down a towel, too, can create a physical distraction.

If you choose to use rose petals, know that they can stain sheets, especially if left overnight. However, the stain is often organic. Generally a couple washings or trip to the dry cleaners will remove the stains from most sheets, depending on the sheet fabric or dyes used in the roses. Rose petals are romantic. If you are not too concerned about potential stains, go for it!

Intimate Sex More Often

Chapter Six
Spruce Up the Bedroom

38. Do not disturb

How many times has sex been better on vacation? Think about it: Fewer distractions help create an environment conducive to creativity and free of pressure. Make sure children are in a safe place outside the room where you are. Leave the animals outdoors, in the garage, in another room, or somewhere else where they will be safe but not disturb you. Turn off your cell phones, and silence or fully disengage your home phone.

39. Keep it comfy

For many people, the ideal temperature is 73º F. (23º C.), but experiment and adjust the room temperature to what's best for both of you. You're trying to avoid the distraction of feeling, "I'm too hot or I'm too cold" and you don't want to be restricted by "covering up" to stay warm. Indoor humidity, if you can control it, is best between

40 and 50 percent. (You can reset everything before going to sleep, as appropriate.)

40. Strip (the bed)
Clean sheets on the bed each time you have sex are best. But when that's not practical, make sure to change your sheets at least weekly (purchase a second set if this makes it more convenient). Use fabric conditioner if you like, and make sure to replace distracting sheets that are stained or torn.

41. Treat yourself like a king or queen
A smaller bed provides more intimacy, but choose a bed size – king, queen, or double – that works for you and your partner's sizes and comfort levels. You may wish to test out different sizes of mattresses at stores or when staying at hotels or friends' homes.

42. Beware of bedposts and rails
Beds without rails and posts allow full play and activity without worry of injury.

43. Once upon a mattress
With notable exceptions, most basic mattresses start to break down after just five years of use. When purchasing a new mattress, do your home-

work to educate yourself on mattress construction, comfort, and longevity. Generally, stick to those with at least 400 coils. Some say latex or innerspring mattresses are best for sex and memory foam is the least favorite. A waterbed may be comfortable for some, but it's not best for achieving intimate sex as often as you might like.

44. Invest in quality bedding

Quality bedding can be expensive, but will last for years – and put you on the road to intimate sex more often in the meantime. It's easy to duplicate luxury hotel experiences at home with items including:

- Boxed, goose down mattress pad cover (a great first acquisition);
- Goose down pillows;
- Goose down blanket with cotton or other natural outer fiber;
- Duvet cover;
- Lightweight, soft, bedspread in a natural-fiber material;
- Long (wide) bedspread or quilt to avoid tucking in sheets on the sides (provides greater freedom);
- At least quarterly cleaning of bedspread (more

frequently if you ever allow a pet on your bed).

Purchase high thread-count sheets. High-quality sheets truly make a difference that will add to your experience. While even higher-count sheets are out there, 800-count sheets (often Egyptian cotton) are your best bet. Make sure you get the "real thing," as some manufacturers may be "cheating" on thread count now that this is becoming a more in-demand consumer item. Some "knock off" sheets have threads tied together to create one thread. Look for sheets on sale from a reputable store. As of the writing of this book, sheets may run from $120 to $290 but are often on sale for $85 to $165. Purchase as a birthday present for yourself, ask for them as a holiday gift, or add them to your registry.

45. Keep it clean

Every component adds visually to the experience. From picking the clothes up off the floor to painting, changing the carpet, or decorating with a theme, your environment will add to your sexual experience. Remember to take away photos of ex-spouses or other sexual partners since your partner may be distracted by these reminders.

46. Turn off the noise

For intimate sex more often, silence (in the room) is golden. Your bedroom should be a place of peace, tranquility, and harmony. Noise can interrupt that tone, so turn off (or remove) TVs, smart phones, computers, PADs, and music (radios, CDs, iPods, and MP3s, etc.). TV often limits or competes with the opportunity for sex (and sleep). If it's on, chances are that one or the other partner is watching or listening to it – and not thinking about his or her partner. Similarly, music, often considered a positive addition, may actually be a distraction during sex. It may lead you to other thoughts (sexual or otherwise), or you might focus on some of the tune's words, thereby losing focus on your partner. Music before or after sex usually does

not distract from an intimate experience. Eliminate other noises by making sure the clock doesn't tick, the air conditioner doesn't clunk, and the fan doesn't make a wobbly noise.

47. Turn on the lights

Over time and as you build trust, agree to turn the lights up, gradually. Add an extra candle, raise a shade, or put the light switch on a dimmer you can adjust. Ideally, you'll have a light switch within reach of the bed (such as a table light). You'll find that adding light heightens your sexual experience by increasing the visual component.

A preference for low lighting during sex is often because someone has a fear or isn't comfortable with him or herself. Talk about it, and as you learn more about the other's concerns, you'll find that he or she will become more open to more light – and to you.

48. It's good to be seen and heard

Since about 70 percent of the population learns and relates visually, sex in the light can be a greatly rewarding experience. For those 30 percent who are more auditory, take care to express yourself fully and don't stifle your vocal cords if at all possible. (Parents might find a kids' overnight at grandparents' or friends' home a welcome event occasionally!) And whether visual or auditory, many women do love to hear their names or hear erotic talk during sex. Again, check with your partner....Learn what he or she likes.

49. Make time stand still

Or at least turn the clocks the other direction. Clocks simply remind you to hurry up and serve as a major distraction. Without a visible clock, you'll be amazed at how quickly time goes by, and by how much quality time you spend together – almost as if it were a dream.

50. Keep it handy

No need for a bedside party, but keep condoms, lubricants, water, and tissues within reach. If you're using condoms, open the package and place at your bedside for easy access. Place lubricants, with the tops off, on either side of the bed so as not to break the continuity. In a new relationship, if more comfortable, place the condoms under the mattress, or under (or inside) a pillow case.

Intimate Sex More Often

Section Two

During Sex

Enhance the Experience

*F*lexibility is the name of the game here. No, that doesn't mean being a gymnast to contort yourself into odd positions. It does mean that maintaining an erotic relationship with a variety of sexual alternatives and scenarios will serve you and your partner well.

Couples who express intimacy (see previous section) through massage, holding hands, bathing together, playful touch, cuddling, and sexual touch have a flexible repertoire and attitude. "Flexible" here is defined as couples who are open to "quickies" as well as long and varied sexual sessions, planned as well as spontaneous encounters, different intercourse positions, and multiple types of stimulation during intercourse.

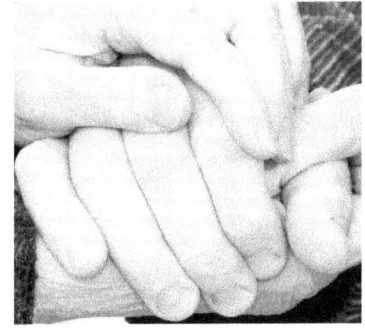

Intimate Sex More Often

Chapter Seven
30 Reliable Ways to Last 4 Times Longer

Men: Read, re-read, then remember this chapter.

51. Be master of your domain

Controlling ejaculation is a learned skill that men can acquire if they decide they want to do so. In learning to do so for 30 minutes or more (yes, 30 minutes), you'll be happier, satisfy your partner more, and gain personal satisfaction and confidence. With patience and learning, you can go six minutes or six hours – at your discretion. Want to learn how? You're not alone. Nearly half the adult male population hasn't learned to control the timing of ejaculation, and surveys say that 95 percent of men under the age of 25 (including most teens) aren't able to do so. Studies indicate that most sexual intercourse that involves thrusting lasts less than 10 minutes, and one in three adult males admit problems with premature ejaculation. No wonder fewer than half of sexual experiences in America today are satisfying to both partners.

In reality, learning control is not that difficult for most men. Since this area is a hot button for so many, let's get into the details. Learning the techniques will get you – and your partner – one (giant) step closer to intimate sex more often.

The first step is to understand the reasons men fall into the trap of not being able to control ejaculation. Then, and only then, can you implement solutions.

Why?

Medical reasons do exist that prevent some men from controlling ejaculation. These range from diabetes, high blood pressure, depression, injury, or as side effects to certain medications. For the vast majority of men, however, it's about attitude, confidence, emotional connection, guilt, anxiety, stigmatization, problems in a relationship, or just habit.

Starting with the teen years, with fear of discovery, men learn to go off fast in the initial stages of sexual discovery and masturbation. When pleasing oneself, there is little or no obvious benefit to lasting longer. Reaching back to the caveman days, men learned that survival from other predators, instilled a need to quickly take care of oneself.

"Old habits die hard," and this area is no exception. Combine the developed habits with pure excitement, natural selfishness, and sheer lack of knowledge on how to do things differently, and you've got quick ejaculation. Those in new relationships will find it's common to go off a little more quickly because of excitement (as partners get to know each other better, things will naturally slow down a bit).

In addition, our bodies (and brains) often confuse anxiety with sexual stimulation. If a man is lacking in sexual confidence in any way, it will impact his ability to control ejaculation. His own sensitivities and anxieties about sex, the relationship, or events in his past — from fears to lingering memories of former experiences or comments — can affect ejaculation.

Other reasons for lack of control include tension in the pelvic area, focus on judging performance rather than enjoying the experience, pressure to "get it over with" (from the woman or the man), and a misunderstanding of the woman's needs.

Don't assume that intercourse is the only thing women want. By now you should understand that generally women need and want more foreplay and more emotional intimacy than men. Men who truly understand this can relax more and find they can control more easily.

Take your time

As you review the following suggestions, keep in mind the ultimate goal: Most experts agree that men consistently need six to seven minutes to climax while women average about 25 minutes. Logically, that tells us that men need to adjust their thinking and methods to learn ways to truly satisfy women for a minimum of 25 minutes (and enjoy it in the process).

Remember, too, that this issue is biological, relational, and psychological – or a combination thereof. It's a multi-faceted issue that can be solved in a number of ways. The important point is that it almost always can be improved. Men reading this with no current partner can implement many of the suggestions on their own, thinking of a future or past relationship partner.

30 Reliable Ways to Last 4 Times Longer

First things first

For those with erection issues, take care of that first. It'll often resolve problems with premature ejaculation and ejaculation control.

1. **Use it or lose it** – The old phrase may apply here. In general, the more regular the sex, the greater the chances are that erection will not be an issue. As a rule, men can keep going until age 80. Before that, it's more a case of men choosing to lose interest.

2. **Go again** – Erections often will return with some stroking; just because you lose it initially doesn't mean your erection is gone for the remainder of the sexual encounter.

3. **Check into external devices** – A cock ring is designed only for maintaining an erection. Your physician can advise on pumps and other devices that may be of help.

4. **Consider medication** – Prescription medications are effective for many. There is plenty of information online or at your local

library. Your physician can advise on if various medications are right for you and on side effects. Medication won't, however, give you better sex, make you a better lover, or make up for what you haven't been doing! It won't replace all the other things in this book, and the relationship between you and your partner. One other interesting note… When reassured by medication, it's believed that many men simply relax more and therefore last longer. Don't disregard the importance of relaxation techniques (see #12 on page 71 in this chapter.)

5. **Get a physical** – If you find you're having problems, see your doctor. You may have circulation issues, and some research even shows that this can be an early warning sign of vascular conditions that can lead to a heart attack or a stroke.

6. **Relate** – Some problems can stem from issues with the relationship itself or issues you have with your partner. Fear, too, can play a part, especially in new relationships.

In some cases, men (or women, for that matter) can't climax with a partner. Yet the erection is there and they can come alone. Along with never thrusting harder and faster (it desensitizes the penis), try a new environment. Don't have sex in bed, switch between intercourse and masturbation, try some sex toys – do what it takes to create a different pattern. Therapy with a sex therapist, counselor, or educator can also help.

Here are some suggestions for extending the sexual experience:

7. **Write** – When both partners write down their perspectives on sex and share it with each other, problems often tend to clear up and the lines of communication (and relaxation) tend to open up.

8. **The point of no return** – By being consciously aware of your own body and knowing your own "point of no return," you can understand that this is not where you want to go.

9. **Go through the phases** – As you learn control, you'll find that you won't move from excitement to climax, but rather from excitement to "maintenance" (or a plateau) in which the body's arousal, and your enjoyment stays level for a while, back to foreplay, and then on to climax. You'll find that this phased approach will enhance your pleasure, not reduce it. Learning to enjoy the excitement and toleration is key to an enhanced sexual experience.

10. **Work as a team** – You'll get better results if you and your partner work together. Make it a joint event, with the right attitude and you'll have fun in the process. Couples who take responsibility for working together to improve ejaculatory control will enhance sexual self-confidence and satisfaction. Just be aware that the change process is usually gradual and requires persistence and patience.

11. **Take it slow** – Many women love the initial penetration. It's one of their favorite moments. Some women may hold back their

enthusiasm because they fear they might excite their partner, causing him to climax too quickly. Sometimes men need to slow down to support this moment – It will benefit both of you.

12. **Relax** – Most people (men and women) have a hard time believing that relaxation is essential for good sex. Letting go of tension, however, will help your body do what you want it to do. It takes the body a few minutes to relax, so when you get into bed or a comfortable position, take time to rest first. And think about it: If you are already anxious or excited when you start sexual activity, what do you think will happen? Countless books and articles are available to detail relaxation techniques. Find what works for you and practice it so it becomes second nature. For starters, if you feel any area of your body tightening up, consciously and pointedly relax those muscles areas, one by one. Don't forget the pelvic muscles, as those are the ones that trigger ejaculation.

Breathe: Shallow breathing works against you. Practice deep breathing.

13. **Take care of her** – Satisfy the woman any number of other ways first. You'll slow yourself down – and allow the intimate experience to evolve to a much higher level.

14. **Withdraw** – Withdraw for 10 seconds and resume activity. Or just stop thrusting for 30 seconds to several minutes, with penetration intact. Move/stroke only occasionally to maintain the erection.

15. **Change positions** – Try starting with the woman on top. Vary the routine.

16. **Be aware** – Learning to be aware of yourself and the sensations you have before, during, and after sex can promote a feeling of relaxation powerful enough to slow things down. The good news is that sexual pleasure has many forms other than orgasm: the sense of touch, the feeling of relaxation in which all your cares and woes are gone for a moment in time, the raw desire and arousal.

17. **Arrange an attitude adjustment** – If your goal is truly to last longer (versus focus on orgasm and instant results), you'll be more likely to achieve it. It's all about attitude.

18. **Take a break** – Talk with your partner about experiencing one or more sexual sessions with the goal of neither climaxing at all. It will truly help you understand how to obtain better control.

19. **It's not a test** – Remember this is meant to be a shared experience of pleasure, not a performance or competition, not about frequency, or proving yourself to a woman. The pressure to perform is only self-defeating. Never obsess on achieving orgasm. Talk about, and lighten up on, any performance expectations, individually and as a couple.

20. **Laugh** – Intimate sex more often is about the relationship between the two of you and enjoying all of each other. Sexual experiences are about what works and need not be everything you see in the latest movie. Laughter provides acceptance and reassurance.

21. **Eliminate the squeeze** – Many experts believe squeezing the head of the penis works only for a very short time, if at all.

22. **Switch it up** – If what you've been doing hasn't worked, change things up! Open up, get out of your comfort zone, and try something different.

23. **Find your style** – Simply knowing what activities provide you extra stimulation, and then consciously reducing them, may help.

then consciously reducing them, may help. Learn your own style by observing what works for you and what doesn't.

24. **Don't take a vacation –** In your mind, anyway. For some people, thinking about something else that makes them smile (baseball, ice cream, the beach, a sunset) creates a distraction and prevents tensing up. But for others, this provides only a temporary solution, if anything.

25. **Double the fun –** Using two condoms may help decrease sensation and help you slow down.

26. **Don't be so sensitive –** Condoms containing numbing ingredients can help slow you down.

27. **Be good to yourself –** Beating yourself up doesn't help. If you're on a learning curve, don't worry if you're not perfect every time. Understand that you lasted longer than your typical time, and eventually, you will gain almost total control. Give yourself a pat on the back: You're working on it!

28. **Exercise** – Almost any form of exercise will make you sharper and more focused, and give you the ability to physically maintain better control. Be cautious of long hours on a bicycle because it can interfere with erection. Some experts say that seven hours a week or more can be a problem. Recumbent bikes, gel-filled seats, and widely available men's-cut seats should help eliminate this problem.

29. **Bring out the toys** – Experiment with sexual toys as a distraction when you want to last longer, but don't become dependent on them.

30. **Visit a sex therapist, educator, counselor, or physician –** If at-home techniques don't work, don't worry. Thousands of specialists reside throughout the country. For a list of licensed professionals visit AASECT.com.

A number of medications on the market can help you last longer, but, as with most things, learning to "do it yourself" is almost always more satisfying (and healthier). If need be, however, discuss drug options with your physician. If you do decide to discuss these issues with your doctor, make sure to take along a full list of any drugs (prescription or other), vitamins, supplements (herbal tea or other), and energy drinks you use.

Even if you've found these suggestions helpful, they only represent a snapshot of what's available. A qualified sex therapist or other professional can work wonders, often very quickly. Don't be shy about seeking help.

Outcomes

If you've read this far, you no doubt realize the positive outcomes of controlling your ejaculation. Your sexual pleasure will increase, your timing will improve as you learn never to go past the

the point of no return, and you'll find that extending the experience will greatly enhance you and your self-confidence.

Perhaps most importantly, you'll move your relationship from ordinary to extraordinary. You'll find you are more comfortable with each other, you'll become closer and stronger as a couple, and you'll look forward to the opportunity to fully experience your partner. Working together, and with longer and longer sexual sessions, will tremendously deepen your intimacy. You'll eliminate any need to say (or feel) apologetic. You'll find you're pleasing your partner in ways neither of you have experienced before, which in turn will make your experience better than you ever imagined.

The ability to control ejaculation provides partners an experience that they cannot imagine otherwise. Whether you have problems in this area, or just want to improve, stay at it and keep the eventual benefits in mind. You, your partner, and your relationship will thank you.

Intimate Sex More Often

Chapter Eight

Explore

52. Position yourself

Learning which positions work best for you and your partner can help maximize your pleasure – especially when one of you is tired or when time is limited. Penis length or thickness, your weight, differences in height, or similar physical factors can influence the positions you use. Get familiar with, and observe, each other's turn-offs as well as turn-ons. It's really a matter of finding what works best for you.

53. Your lucky number

Remember, for both men and women, achieving multiple orgasms – whether two, three, seven, or more – is a learned experience. For men, once comfortable, you'll find you don't have to ejaculate all at once. You'll be able to save some for later, possibly enabling you to achieve multiple ejaculations in the same sexual encounter.

Men also need to remember that lasting longer can allow the woman to get to a much better place. Unlike men, when a woman is wet, it doesn't mean that she is ready emotionally or physiologically. Remember that the woman needs, on average, about four times as long as men.

****
Men, you don't have to ejaculate all at once....Save some for later, enabling you to achieve multiple ejaculations in the same sexual encounter.

Women, technically there is no limit to the number of orgasms you can have in any given sexual experience.
****

According to one sex therapist interviewed, many women don't realize, believe, or understand that they can have multiple orgasms and therefore stop after one. Technically, there is no limit to the number of orgasms women can have in any given sexual experience; it's more a matter of when a woman tires. For most couples, becoming familiar with what works will enable the woman to experience more multiple orgasms.

Women who have never climaxed, and think they are unable to, will likely find that the tips in this book will lead to success. It's about getting to know oneself, and communicating with your partner, to find and implement what works. Adopt an open attitude to experiment and learn what works for you. Let your partner know what that is and when it's happening. Provide some direction and guidance, realizing your partner probably can't read minds. Above all, when something is working, keep doing it to achieve multiple orgasms. Afterward, talk about it: what worked and why?

54. Experiment

Exploring every square inch of his or her body or being explored can be intoxicating. Learn how to touch and what response you get from different acts.

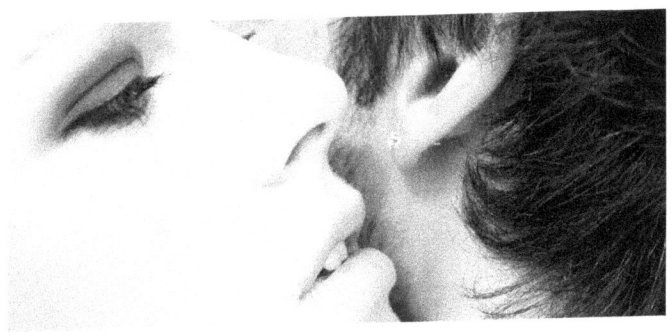

To keep things fresh and interesting, vary positions, speed, and intensity, and create variety. There's only one rule: Any activity that you both enjoy is not kinky; repeating an activity that only one of you enjoys is kinky and can build resentment and perhaps diminish sexual interest.

55. Head-to-toe
Talk and caress lying in opposite directions. This often-pleasing, visual experience helps build and confirm confidence in each other.

56. A couple that plays together...
You may not engage in joint masturbation often, but it will help each of you to learn more about what works for the other. It's simply one more technique that will bring you closer to intimate sex, more often.

57. Sweat!
Instead of fearing it, make the most of it! If one of you sweats, let it work for both of you by using it as you would an oil. Slide your bodies against each other.

Explore

Periodically, stop and talk with your partner to be sure things are comfortable....If you sense something is off a bit, you'll likely be right. Pay attention to what's going on.

Chapter Nine
Check In

58. What's up

Periodically stop and talk with your partner to be sure things are comfortable: not too rough, slow, or fast, and that nothing is causing pain or discomfort. You may just need a break or more lubricant, but pay attention to the little things. If you sense something is off a bit, you'll likely be right. Pay attention to what's going on. Slow down, take a break, and make sure not to force anything. Is there an elephant in the room? (See Chapter 25) Is your partner drying a bit? Maybe it's because of an antihistamine she's taking for an allergy. If she's experiencing pain, it may be a subject about which she needs to talk with her physician. Realize it may or may not have anything to do with you. But do talk about it and ask questions to figure out what's up.

59. Fantasize

Exchange thoughts regarding your fantasies, too. Let your partner know of yours, and ask about his or hers. You can eliminate worries about what your partner may think by simply asking up-front.

Don't mind read....Ask, communicate, support each other. If helpful, consciously switch concentration from yourself to your partner.

Chapter Ten
Relax

60. Operate on autopilot
As you better understand the ingredients to intimate sex, you'll be able to implement many actions and suggestions automatically.

61. Take a breath
Take a few deep breaths frequently during your sexual experience to promote relaxation and enjoyment.

62. (Don't) mind-read
Each individual has a responsibility to get what he or she wants and needs. As much as you try to give to your partner, remember that you can't second-guess what s/he needs. Ask, communicate, support each other. Then consciously switch concentration from yourself to your partner every few minutes.

63. It's not everything
Sex isn't about intercourse or performance. It's about shared closeness, emotional intimacy, how you and your partner feel, and how you make each other feel. Neither of you need to have a cli-

max or orgasm. Your sexual experience can be wonderful without it.

Men, there's no need to feel guilty about not being able to ejaculate, nor worry if the woman is satisfied but doesn't have a climax. Truly satisfying a woman is the ultimate personal satisfaction. To know that you can bring so much pleasure and happiness to someone else, and that you are one of the few who can, produces a deep level of confidence only a few men will ever know.

64. Come together (or not)

Focusing on synchronized climax takes away from the experience, as you're unable to focus completely on the moment. And no matter what you read in novels, the truth is that it rarely happens.

65. Lose your inhibitions

The more comfortable you become with yourself, your partner, and your mutual communication, the more you'll try or discuss new things.

Relax

Men, there's no need to feel guilty about not being able to ejaculate, nor worry if the woman is satisfied but doesn't have a climax. These things are not important. The ultimate personal satisfaction is truly satisfying a woman. If you are one of the few who can do it, you will experience a level of confidence deeper than most men will ever know.

If you went to a restaurant week after week and never told the waiter what you wanted, you'd likely get standard fare. With some direct communication, your experience would improve. The same is true of your sexual experience.

Section Three
After Sex
Finish Strong

At the beginning of the book, we likened communication to dining at a great restaurant. If you went to the restaurant week after week and never told the waiter what you wanted, you'd likely get standard fare. With some direct communication, your dining experience would improve. The same is true of your sexual experience.

By now, I hope you've magnified your sexual dining experience by talking more with your partner and learning what the two of you want and need from sex – and from life. I hope you're now looking forward to creating experiences rather than just having sex.

The good news is that when sex is over, it's not quite over. There's more to enjoy. Afterplay and afterglow will be new concepts to many men and women…Keep reading to find out more.

Intimate Sex More Often

Chapter Eleven
Bask in the Afterglow

66. Engage in afterplay
Men, if you went off first, make sure to take care of your partner's physical needs afterwards.

67. Go again
If it's been a good session and for a good period of time, many men can go again in as little as 30 seconds, if the penis is half-limp. Waiting until the penis goes fully limp generally means waiting for a longer period of time. How long? It could be a minute or two for younger men, 30-60 minutes for middle-aged men, or a day or two for an 80-year-old.

68. 15 minutes of fame
Experience at least 15 minutes of afterglow together. Sometimes you will be physically exhausted, even to the point where it's hard to walk. This will be memorable sex! Enjoy your time together. Try not to break the continuity by going to the bathroom, grabbing a tissue, or even taking

off the condom. According to many experts, the length of the sexual afterglow stage will be related to the length of plateau (maintenance) stage.

69. Snuggle
After sex, don't simply get up, roll over, or go to sleep without checking in with your partner.

70. Pack a toothbrush
Whenever possible, stay together for the rest of the day or night.

71. Love means never having to say you're sorry
Never thank or apologize for anything in the sexual experience. Both type of comments cheapen the experience. Do, however, talk about how you felt, what you liked, and what you'd like to do next time.

72. Sleep naked
Sleeping naked with your partner is not only sensual, but reassuring, satisfying, and confidence-building. Once you're used to it, you'll never go back to pajamas!

73. Just a touch

Touch – in some way – all night long. A finger here, a toe there, the top of one foot under the sole of the other…All will give you an inner peace that lasts the entire next day. You'll find that you won't lose sleep, but come in and out of deep sleep cycles aware of touching or being retouched. To enhance the experience, try this small, but pleasure-inducing trick: Place the heaviest extremity on bottom. So, for example, place a lighter, smaller finger on top of the heavier one when touching your partner.

74. 24 hours

Keep the experience in your mind, and heart, for 24 hours. If you're still marveling at the experience emotionally and physically, you're doing great.

75. The day after

Discuss the experience later or the next day. Be sensitive, but do discuss in an emotionally safe environment. Remember: Communication is what intimate sex, more often is all about! You cannot second-guess what is working or not.

Whether or not you agree or disagree with the ideas in this book, I hope I've planted a seed of discussion for you and your partner resulting in communication that will help you achieve intimate sex more often!

Afterword

My personal goal is for you, my reader, to take the information presented here and use it to bring more satisfaction and fulfillment to your life. I hope you move through your day with an unspoken glow others can see. By putting into practice a new attitude, outlook, and perhaps a technique or two, you will improve your relationships, your happiness, and your sexual experiences. And whether or not you agree or disagree with a given idea or thought, perhaps I've planted a seed of discussion for you and your partner.

The result: Communication that will help you achieve intimate sex more often. You'll enjoy the inner peace that comes when you know you've done your best and when you've experienced the greatest pleasure.

If you want help in finding some of the items mentioned in the book, checking out some of the best resources, or just want to expand your sexual education, check out:
www.IntimateSexMoreOften.com.

And do let me know what a difference this book has made in your life. I'd like to hear from you.

Dave Robin
Dave@IntimateSexMoreOften.com

Share a Book with a Friend

*Order a book today
so that you can share the 75 enlightening
tips in "Intimate Sex More Often"
with someone you love*

YES, I want _____ copies of *Intimate Sex More Often* at $8.98 each, plus $4 shipping and handling. (Colorado residents please include $1.00 sales tax.)

Name_____

Address_____

City/State/Zip_____

Phone_____Email_____

❑ Check enclosed • Charge my   ❑ VISA   ❑ MasterCard

Card #_____Exp._____

Signature_____

Visit www.IntimateSexMoreOften.com

Mail your check and order form to:
Diamond Publications
6655 W Jewell Ave, #218
Lakewood, CO 80232

www.ingramcontent.com/pod-product-compliance
Lightning Source LLC
Chambersburg PA
CBHW071301040426
42444CB00009B/1812